The Radical Prayer

To order additional copies of

The Radical Prayer,

by Derek J. Morris,

call 1-800-765-6955.

Visit us at

www.AutumnHousePublishing.com

for information on other Autumn House® products.

The Radical Prayer

Derek J. Morris

Special thanks for
developmental funding

JUDITH A. THOMAS

Ministerial Association

Autumn
House® Publishing
www.autumnhousepublishing.com
A Division of **REVIEW AND HERALD® PUBLISHING**
Since 1861

Published by Autumn House® Publishing, a division of Review and Herald® Publishing, Hagerstown, MD 21741-1119

This book was
Edited by Gerald Wheeler
Copyedited by James Cavil
Designed by Trent Truman
Cover photos by istock
Typeset: Clearface 10/20

PRINTED IN U.S.A.

12 11 10 09 08   5 4 3 2 1

Library of Congress Cataloging-in-Publication Data
Morris, Derek John, 1954-   .
  The radical prayer : will you respond to the appeal of Jesus? / Derek J. Morris.
      p. cm.
  1. Witness bearing (Christianity)—Biblical teaching. 2. Prayer—Biblical
teaching. I. Title.
  BS2545.W54M67 2008
  248.3'2--dc22

                        2008010893

ISBN 978-0-8127-0486-0 Hardcover
ISBN 978-0-8127-0487-7 Paperback

This book is

Dedicated

to all who have responded
to the appeal of Jesus.

Like great men and women of God
through the ages,
you have courageously prayed the radical prayer.

In Praise of Radical Prayer

Derek Morris's Radical Prayer is powerful material, a must-read for all those who want a closer walk with God. I am convinced that when we give the Lord of the harvest primacy in our lives, He will give us the Spirit's power to change the world. As you read these pages, open your heart to a renewed experience with the Lord of the harvest.

—Mark Finley, Evangelist

Why are we here? Not just to function in our own little world but to advance God's kingdom. That's what The Radical Prayer is all about. This book is not just for pastors and evangelists but for everyone who has accepted Christ as Savior and Lord and anticipates His soon return.

—Jack Blanco, Th.D., Retired Dean of Theology
Ooltewah, Tennessee

Acknowledgments

I want to express my appreciation to the numerous individuals who have provided encouragement and assistance in completing this book:

To Jack Blanco, James Cress, Robert Folkenberg, and Gordon Retzer—people used by the Lord of the harvest to encourage me to put these thoughts into print.

To Janis Lowry, Don Mansell, Eve Parker, and Nancy Vasquez—who provided invaluable feedback in the shaping and editing of the manuscript.

To my beloved wife, Bodil—who patiently supported me during the writing process and prayed for me.

Each of these individuals, along with others unnamed, encouraged me to be attentive to the steady conviction of God's Spirit.

Most of all, I want to give thanks and honor to the Lord of the harvest, who has saved me by His grace, empowers me by His Spirit, and continues to use me in His harvest. "To God our Savior, who alone is wise, be glory and majesty, dominion and power, both now and forever. Amen" (Jude 25).

Contents

Introduction

All too often we simply pray weak prayers, such as "Dear God, help me to have a nice day" and "Help me not to get so angry today." However, Jesus challenges each one of His followers to pray a radical prayer. It's a short prayer, but it's certainly not weak. In fact, it's a powerful prayer.

If you want to maintain the status quo, don't even begin this prayer. Or if you want to live an average life, leave it alone. But if you have a passion to make a difference in the world—if you have a longing to see Jesus return in glory as King of kings and Lord of lords—then I invite you to learn more about this radical prayer.

Once you begin to pray this radical prayer in faith, the way will open for great and wonderful things to happen. Your life will truly be transformed, and you will never be the same again. Are you ready? Then read on.

1

Seeing the World From a Radical Perspective

I love mountains! I can still remember the very first time I rode in a cable car up the side of a rugged snow-covered slope. The view was exhilarating. However, when I finally reached the top of the mountain and stepped out of the cable car, my whole perspective changed. Now, instead of merely gazing at one snow-covered mountainside, I had an amazing panoramic view of a whole range of majestic snow-covered mountains. That moment will remain in my memory forever. I was seeing the world from a new viewpoint!

The Radical Perspective

God wants *you* to view the world from a new perspective. Not just from a different altitude. He longs for you to see the world as He does—from a divine perspective. A radical perspective! Once you have caught a glimpse of God's radical perspective, then you will be ready to learn about the radical prayer.

So what is this radical perspective? It is found in Luke 10:2. Jesus shares with His disciples, and also with us, that "the harvest truly is great." What does Jesus mean when He says that the harvest truly is plentiful, abundant, and extensive? Scripture employs the metaphor of the harvest in two ways. First, Jesus uses the imagery of the harvest when referring to the end of the world. In Matthew 13:39 He tells us: "The harvest is the end of the age, and the reapers are the angels." Revelation 14:15 employs it in a similar manner: "Thrust in Your sickle and reap, for the time has come for You to reap, for the harvest of the earth is ripe." These two passages make it clear that the harvest can refer to the gathering of the saints at the end of the age and to the judgment of the wicked.

But Jesus also uses the metaphor of the harvest to refer to present missionary endeavors, that is, leading men and women to a saving knowledge of the Lord Jesus Christ and gathering them into the kingdom of God. This is the meaning of the harvest in Luke 10:2. Consider the context. In Luke 10:1 Luke tells us: "After these things the Lord appointed seventy others also, and sent them two by two before His face into every city and place where He Himself was about to go." A present activity, it is not the final harvest at the end of the world. In His present harvest work God employs people, not angels. Jesus is sending His disciples out, two by two, into God's harvest.

So what does He want us to understand when He says that the harvest truly is great? Simply this: many people—men and women, boys and girls—are ready and waiting to be gathered into His kingdom. They only need to hear the good news and receive the invitation. According to Jesus, there is a present harvest to bring in, and it "truly is great."

Why does Jesus emphasize the magnitude of the harvest? Because it is great! On the day of Pentecost, when the apostles witnessed the conversion of 3,000 individuals, I'm sure that they said to each other, *"The harvest truly is great!"* When we see thousands receiving Christ as Savior and Lord, we also find it easy to repeat the same thing to one another. The words of Jesus are obviously true.

"Lift up your eyes and look at the fields, for they are already white for harvest!"

But at times it might not appear as if the harvest will amount to anything at all. From a human perspective, it can seem as if crop failure has struck. At those times, Jesus still urges us to remember the immensity of the harvest. He urges us to view reality from a radical perspective. When we see as He does, we will discover that the harvest truly *is* great.

A Great Harvest at Sychar

Have you ever read the story of Jesus meeting with the Samaritan woman at the well of Sychar (John 4:3-42)? At first glance, there doesn't seem to be much of a harvest of souls there. Jesus encounters only one person—just one wayward woman. When the disciples arrive on the scene, they immediately evaluate the situation and conclude, *There's not much of a harvest here.* Jesus discerns their thoughts and reads their faces. Then He startles them by declaring, "Do you not say, 'There are still four months and then comes the harvest'? Behold, I say to you, lift up your eyes and look at the fields, for they are already white for harvest" (John 4:35).

In spite of the bleak landscape, Jesus sees that the harvest truly is *great*. That once-wayward woman returns to Sychar and gives her testimony about her life-changing encounter with the Messiah. Many Samaritans believe in Jesus because of her witness. The harvest is so plentiful that Jesus stays for two extra days, and many more become believers because of His words.

Some of us would probably have driven straight through

town without stopping. Or better yet, we might have chosen to avoid the town completely. No harvest here. At least not one that we can see from a human perspective. But Jesus challenges us to look again—to open our eyes. Or perhaps to give the Lord of the harvest permission to open our eyes and enable us to see from His radical perspective. Then we will more fully comprehend His words: *"The harvest truly is great."*

A Great Harvest at Sybertsville

I conducted my first public meetings in the small, economically depressed town of Sybertsville, Pennsylvania. I was young and inexperienced, but the faithful followers of Jesus in that community were most encouraging. We rented a fire hall and sent out some invitations.

Realizing that I needed some powerful messages, I called a well-known Christian evangelist and asked if I could borrow his sermons. When he agreed, I knew right then that God was at work. I spent about 400 hours transcribing those messages and making them my own.

As we prepared for the meetings, we had no idea if anyone would even show up on opening night. But somehow we had courage to believe the words of Jesus: *"The harvest truly is great."* That first night the fire hall was full! The Lord of the harvest blessed as He always does when we put our trust in Him. I learned an important lesson during the next five weeks. It doesn't matter what people say. You often hear: "It can't happen here." Or "It won't work." Or "No one will show up." But I learned that when the Lord of the harvest is involved, anything can happen anywhere. It is His harvest—not ours. The Lord of the harvest knows what He is doing.

Small Response—Big Harvest

On the day that the mob stoned Stephen to death, he didn't notice much of a harvest as a result of his preaching. The Bible tells us that most of the people in the audience were furious, gnashing their teeth, covering their ears, ranting and raving—not exactly a positive response from his listeners. But Jesus looked down from the right hand of the throne of God and said, "The harvest truly is great."

A young man by the name of Saul of Tarsus was in charge of the coats that day. The witness of Stephen changed Saul's life forever. Not long after hearing Stephen's sermon, Saul of Tarsus fell flat on his face before the risen Christ on the road to Damascus and cried out, "Lord, what do You want me to do?" (Acts 9:6). Stephen's final sermon, preached through both his life and his death, would through Saul touch the lives of thousands of future followers of the Lord Jesus Christ. Jesus was right—the harvest truly *is* great, even when it may not be immediately apparent to us.

As a young pastor I witnessed a similar miracle. I had the privilege of participating in some public meetings in Allentown, Pennsylvania. Our team sensed the Spirit of God in our midst, but not too many visitors attended those sessions. Only a few people made decisions to become fully devoted followers of Jesus. From a human perspective, one might have concluded that the harvest wasn't that great. Maybe Jesus had made a mistake this time. There was, however, one young couple named

Gary and Laurie who came faithfully night by night. They seemed extremely interested in the truths of God's Word. But by the end of the series they just didn't feel convicted to make a complete commitment to Jesus Christ as their Savior and Lord. Have you ever met anyone like that? It looked as if we had a total crop failure.

All we could do now was pray. After all, the Lord of the harvest was the one in charge. On Friday afternoon, as Gary left work and drove down the highway toward home, he came under the overwhelming conviction of the Holy Spirit that God wanted him to make a complete surrender of his life to Jesus Christ and to acknowledge that decision through baptism. Gary had no doubt in his mind. He only wondered how

he would share the news with his wife, Laurie. But by the time he arrived home, he discovered that the Lord of the harvest had been there before him.

They seemed extremely interested in the truths of God's Word.

That same afternoon, as Gary headed home, his wife, Laurie, sat in their house. She also came under the overwhelming conviction of the Holy Spirit that God wanted her to make the same life commitment. Imagine their surprise and joy when they shared their decision with each other. And imagine *our* surprise and joy when they told us the following day!

Perhaps you're thinking, *It's wonderful that two people made a complete commitment to Jesus Christ, were baptized, and became fully devoted followers of Jesus. But that's hardly a great harvest!* You might be right—if you were evaluating the situation from a human perspective. But the Lord of the harvest knew that the rest of the story had not yet been told. That young couple, Gary and Laurie, sensed the call of God to enter into full-time ministry. Even though Laurie was struggling with a terminal disease, they courageously followed the call of God. Gary, who had been working in a factory that assembled catalytic converters, left his former occupation and studied to become a pastor. Now, instead of helping to convert exhaust fumes, he is helping to convert people. And instead of just making a living, he is being used by the Lord of the harvest to make a difference.

The Lord of the harvest is in the miracle-working business. Gary is still serving in full-time ministry. Thousands have heard the truth about Jesus as a result of his testimony. Was the harvest *great?* Absolutely! The words of Jesus are true, my friends. Even though it may not always be clear to us, the harvest truly is *great.*

The Lord of the harvest wants you to see the world from His radical perspective. He longs to use you to gather in His harvest. But first you must recognize a radical problem.

2

Recognizing a Radical Problem

Jesus identifies a radical problem for the Lord of the harvest: "The harvest truly is great, but the laborers are few" (Luke 10:2). Why are there so few laborers? Perhaps an inadequate number of them were assigned. In that case, we could blame the Lord of the harvest. He should have anticipated the size of the task. If He knew that the harvest was going to be abundant, He should have assigned a large enough crew. Maybe it's His fault that the laborers are few. What do you think?

Too Few *Laboring* Laborers

Ask yourself an important question: How many individuals has the Lord of the harvest called to be laborers in His harvest? If you answered, "Everyone who chooses to become a part of His kingdom," you're right! Jesus' command to preach the gospel to every person on earth involved more than just the 11 remaining disciples. When He said, "Go therefore and make disciples of all the nations, baptizing them in the name of the Father and of the Son and of the Holy Spirit" (Matt. 28:19), He meant that instruction for all of us—for everyone who accepts the call to become part of the kingdom of heaven.

If God summons all of us to participate in the Lord's harvest, perhaps our initial question should be modified. Instead of asking, "Why are there so few laborers?" we should rather inquire, "Why are there so few *laboring* laborers?" Most of the so-called laborers seem to be inactive. "The harvest truly is great, but the *laboring* laborers are few."

Distracted Laborers

Perhaps one explanation for the sparse number of laborers reaping the Lord's harvest is that some of us laborers have become distracted. Don't we care whether people are saved or lost? Are we deliberately turning a deaf ear to the appeal of the Lord of the harvest? Have we let less important things capture our attention?

Jesus told the story of a man who had two sons. This father asked them to work in his vineyard—to be reapers in his harvest. One refused, but later regretted his hasty decision and went. The second son initially agreed to go, but didn't (Matt. 21:28-30). Have you ever wondered why the second son didn't work in his father's vineyard? Do you think he was lying to his father, deliberately trying to deceive him? I doubt it. He probably intended to go—after all, it was the right thing to do. But somehow someone or something else captured his attention, and before he knew it, the day had slipped away. The story leaves us wondering what might have caused him to become a nonlaboring laborer.

In another story, Jesus told about some guests invited to a great banquet. They weren't expected to do any labor. They just had to show up and enjoy the party, but they also became distracted. If you read the story, you'll discover some of the excuses they made:

"How then will the great harvest be gathered in?"

"A certain man gave a great supper and invited many, and sent his servant at supper time to say to those who were invited, 'Come, for all things are now ready.'

"But they all with one accord began to make excuses. The first said to him, 'I have bought a piece of ground, and I must go and see it. I ask you to have me excused.'

"And another said, 'I have bought five yoke of oxen, and I am going to test them. I ask you to have me excused.'

"Still another said, 'I have married a wife, and therefore I cannot come'" (Luke 14:16-20).

Do you notice the distractions? Material possessions—a piece of land. Business activity—trying out a new pair of oxen. Relationships—the person just got married. Now, there's nothing inherently wrong with material possessions, business activity, or relationships. But when any of them get in the way of God's invitation, we have a real problem.

Discouraged Laborers

A second possible explanation that so few *laboring* laborers participate in the Lord's harvest is that some have become discouraged. After all, the task is enormous. Because the harvest truly *is* great it's easy to feel overwhelmed.

We can suggest several reasons a laborer might become discouraged. One might be trying to bring in the harvest all by himself or herself. I have met some laborers who struggle unceasingly until they're exhausted. They give their all and then some, but it never seems enough.

May I remind you that the Lord of the harvest doesn't expect you to work yourself into an early grave? Just as did the early disciples of Jesus, you need to take time to go apart and rest awhile (Mark 6:30, 31). But you ask, "How then will the great harvest be gathered in?" The apostles faced a similar challenge in the early days of the Christian church. The immensity of the task overwhelmed them. And so, guided by the Holy Spirit, they delegated responsibility to others. God does not demand that you do everything by yourself. Make room for others to work by your side.

You may also become discouraged because you are trying to bring in the harvest in your own strength. If you try to serve the Lord of the harvest trusting in your own resources, you will surely become discouraged. We all need to live by the words of the prophet Zechariah: "'Not by might nor by power, but by My Spirit,' says the Lord of hosts" (Zech. 4:6). Otherwise, you will surely become a discouraged, nonlaboring laborer.

The Transformation of Simon Peter

At this point you may be thinking, *This is* a radical *problem! There are too few* laboring *laborers. Too many of the professed followers of Jesus have become distracted and discouraged.* But there is good news! The Lord of the harvest can take nonlaboring, distracted, discouraged laborers and renew them by His grace, empower them by His Spirit, and send them out as focused, effective harvesters.

Consider the experience of Simon Peter, one of Christ's first followers. He had listened to the words of Jesus when He sent the twelve and later the 70 out: "The harvest truly is great, but the laborers are few" (Luke 10:2). Simon Peter had experienced the power of the Lord of the harvest as he labored in Jesus' name. He healed the sick, set the oppressed free, and preached the good news with power. But Simon Peter became distracted by his own failures and discouraged by his own frailty. How did Jesus respond? Instead of giving up on him, Jesus called Simon Peter again, renewed him by His grace, and empowered him by His Spirit. That distracted and discouraged disciple experienced a personal transformation. He became bold—not in his own strength, but by the Spirit of God. Simon Peter became focused and fearless. Once again he began to labor boldly in the Lord's harvest and gathered in thousands of men and women. If Jesus can take a distracted, discouraged person such as Simon Peter and transform him into a focused, effective laborer in the Lord's harvest, then He can do that for other distracted and discouraged nonlaboring laborers. He can do the same thing for me, and He can do it for you.

> *"The harvest truly is great, but the laborers are few" (Luke 10:2).*

The Transformation of Simon Madrigal

Some years ago another young man named Simon entered my office. He had spent his teenage years in East Los Angeles. The Lord Jesus Christ rescued this young man from a life of violence and crime and called him to be a laborer in the Lord's harvest. Simon had already seen God work in his life in marvelous ways, but he had become distracted and discouraged—not by the present, but by the past. Some nights he sat on his bed looking at his gang tattoos, wondering, *Can God really use me, after all I've done?* He was a classic example of a modern distracted and discouraged laborer.

As Simon sat in my office, tears filled his eyes and rolled down his cheeks like liquid prayers. As I listened to his heart-cry, God gave me a word of hope for him. "We don't have to stay where we are," I explained. "Nor are we bound by what we used to be." Simon embraced the good news of God's Word. Divine grace renewed him, and the Spirit of God empowered him. Just a few weeks later, as Simon was sharing the good news about Jesus with others, God impressed him to tell his life story. Until then he had been too ashamed to tell it in public. But not anymore! At the end of his testimony Simon gave a simple invitation, and 15 people received Jesus Christ as their personal Savior and Lord.

A few days later Simon received a call from a Christian mission organization asking him to serve on a mission team in South America. He worked in the city of Salvador, in northeast Brazil, visiting people in parts of the city to which not only the locals were afraid to go but even the police refused to enter. God even used Simon's old gang tattoos to earn him a little respect among the local gang members. As a result of those meetings, 5,000 people chose to become fully dedicated followers of Jesus.

Since then Simon has devoted his life to telling people about Jesus. Although he still remembers his past and still bears the scars, he now rejoices that God can take distracted, discouraged, nonlaboring laborers and turn them into focused, effective laborers in His harvest. That transformation occurred because Simon was willing to pray a *radical* prayer.

So what was his radical prayer? He responded to the appeal that Jesus makes in Luke 10:2. Now that you have caught

a glimpse of God's radical perspective—that *"the harvest truly is great"*—and you recognize the radical problem of too few *laboring* laborers, you are ready to learn about the radical prayer that Jesus wants you to pray.

3

Praying the Radical Prayer

We have seen the radical perspective: the harvest truly is great. And we have also recognized the radical problem: there are too few *laboring* laborers. So where do we go from here? Jesus challenges us to pray a radical prayer.

Bold Prayers

Have you ever prayed a bold prayer? I do not have in mind the standard blessing at the meal table, "Thank You for the world so sweet, thank You for the food we eat," or the run of the mill "Now I lay me down to sleep, I pray the Lord my soul to keep." Rather, I'm talking about a bold prayer.

Elijah stretched himself out three times over the lifeless body of the son of the widow of Zarephath and prayed, "O Lord my God, I pray, let this child's soul come back to him" (1 Kings 17:21). That was a bold prayer.

Jesus, when He held a small lunch in His hands, prayed to His heavenly Father to provide food for a vast multitude (Mark 6:41). That was also a bold prayer. The Gospel writers don't give us the exact words of Jesus' prayer that day, but I know He wasn't just saying, "Thank You for the world so sweet, thank You for the food we eat." No, Jesus offered a bold prayer.

The Radical Prayer

Now Jesus challenges you to pray a bold prayer. Dare I say a *radical* prayer? Listen to the words of Jesus: "The harvest truly is great, but the laborers are few; *therefore pray the Lord of the harvest to send out laborers into His harvest*" (Luke 10:2).

At first glance this may not sound like a radical prayer—but read on. A careful study of His words will reveal that it is indeed a startling request. Several Greek verbs can be translated "pray." Is Jesus asking us to make a request? to express a desire? No! It's more intense than that. The Greek verb used here, *deomai*, means "to beseech," "to plead earnestly," "to beg." Do you sense the intensity of that word? It is so much stronger than simply "to pray."

Let's consider some passages that employ *deomai*. We find it twice in connection with Jesus' teaching on how to pray to the Lord of the harvest. It also appears in Luke 5:12 in connection with a leper begging for healing, in Luke 8:38 in which a man freed from a legion of demons pleads to go with Jesus, and in Luke 9:38 in which a father longs for his son's deliverance from an evil spirit. Do any of those occurrences seem as if they were simply expressing a desire or making a request? What does it sound like to you?

Perhaps even more helpful for our understanding of *de-omai* is the use of the verb in Luke 22:31, 32: "Simon, Simon! Indeed, Satan has asked for you, that he may sift you as wheat. But I have *prayed* for you, that your faith should not fail." The disciple faced the danger of eternal loss. How do you think Jesus prayed for Peter? The answer is in the text. The verb is *deomai*. It was an intense prayer. Jesus *earnestly pleaded* with the Father on Simon Peter's behalf. That's how Jesus tells us to pray the radical prayer. Pray intensely. Beg.

The Earnest Appeal of Jesus

Notice this verb is in the imperative: "therefore *pray* the Lord of the harvest . . ." What does the use of an imperative imply? It's a command, or an appeal. An imperative expects an active response. Should a firefighter run into a public building and shout, "Vacate this building immediately," it is not a polite suggestion. It's an order. Or if teachers say to their students, "Turn in your homework at the end of class," it's not just a tentative request. They expect an active response.

Similarly, when Jesus says to the disciples—and also to

us—"Pray," He is assuming that we will respond. But there's even more that we can learn from these words of Jesus. Greek can state the imperative in two ways. A present imperative has the idea of "keep on doing what you're already doing." Should you be running away from a mad dog, and I shout, "Run! Run!" I would use a present imperative. In other words, you are running; now, just keep on running. Similarly, when Jesus says in Matthew 7:7, "Ask, and it will be given to you," He uses a present imperative. Jesus is saying, "You are already asking. Continue to ask. Keep on asking."

"But I have prayed for you, that your faith should not fail."

But Greek also has an *aorist* imperative, which can convey the meaning of "start doing something that you're not yet doing." If I'm standing in a ditch, leaning on my shovel, and the boss says, "Dig!" he means, "Start digging! You're not digging now, but you need to start doing it." That would be an *aorist* imperative in Greek. Similarly, when Jesus tells the people at Lazarus' tomb, "Loose him, and let him go" (John 11:44), He uses an *aorist* imperative. "You're not yet unwrapping him. Look at him. He's all bound up, and he can't free himself. Start unwrapping him and let him go." Do you see the difference?

In His appeal for us to pray a radical prayer, Jesus asks us to pray earnestly—to plead, to beg. By using an *aorist* imperative, He is saying to us, "Start praying earnestly. You're not yet praying as you should. Instead, you need to start pleading with the Lord of the harvest."

At this point, you might be thinking, *Wait a minute! I don't understand. Why do I need to beg the Lord of the harvest to send out laborers? Why do I need to start pleading with Him as I've never prayed before? Doesn't the Lord of the harvest already want to do this?* Absolutely. So why then do we need to beg? Let me suggest that it has more to do with changing our hearts than God's. We are giving Him permission to do something radical.

Throwing Out Laborers

What, then, is so radical about this prayer? As we dig deeper, we find the answer in the words of Jesus. We are to plead earnestly with the Lord of the harvest to do what? "Send out laborers into His harvest." That doesn't sound very radical. But "send out laborers" is not an accurate translation of the Greek. The common verb in Greek for "send out" is *apostellō,* from which we get the noun *apostolos,* "apostle." When the Gospels record that Jesus "sent out" the disciples, they use the verb *apostellō.* But the verb Jesus employs in Luke 10:2 is much more radical.

"Send out laborers" isn't even an accurate translation. It's far too polite. The verb used here is *ekballō. Ballō* means "to cast" or "to throw." The Gospel writer John employs *ballō* when the disciples cast their nets out of the ship (John 21:6), when the enemies of Jesus picked up rocks to hurl at Him (John 8:59), and when Herod had John the Baptist thrown into prison (John 3:24). Thus *ballō* means to throw or cast. But that still doesn't capture the complete meaning of Jesus' radical prayer.

The Greek verb He used in Luke 10:2 is *ekballō*. The prefix ek stands for "out." So *ekballō* means "to throw out," or "to cast out." On numerous occasions the Gospels employ *ekballō* for casting out demons. The verb *ekballō* also occurs when Jesus drove the money changers out of the Temple (John 2:15). As you can see, it is not a weak verb, and Jesus is not asking you to pray a flimsy prayer. What He is asking you to do is to plead with the Lord of the harvest "to throw out" laborers, "to hurl out" laborers, "to cast out" laborers into His harvest. That is a radical prayer!

When the Lord of the harvest throws you out, He is not discarding you.

A Personal Request

You can't possibly pray this radical prayer unless you're willing to be a part of the answer to it. Let me put this radical prayer into simple words:

"Lord of the harvest, I earnestly beg You to throw out laborers into Your harvest, and You have my permission to begin with *me.*"

Jesus Himself was willing to be thrown out! Matthew records that immediately after His baptism the Spirit led Him into the wilderness. Later Jesus emerged from that wilderness to begin His active ministry, in fulfillment of the prophecy of the prophet Isaiah. The Gospel writer Mark, on the other hand, records that Jesus was "thrown out" by the Spirit. Most translators don't render the Greek accurately. The verb in Mark 1:12 is *ekballō.* Jesus was willing to be thrown out into the harvest. Jesus was willing to pray a radical prayer.

Perhaps you're thinking, *What will happen to me if I give the Lord of the harvest permission to throw me out into His harvest?* That is His responsibility, not yours. When the Lord of the harvest throws you out, He is not discarding you. Rather, He is placing you where He wants you to be. It may be a distant land, or it may be right where you currently live. Your assignment—my assignment—is to be willing, to be ready, to pray the radical prayer, to earnestly plead: "Lord of the harvest, I earnestly beg You to throw out laborers into Your harvest, and You have my permission to begin with *me.*" Are you willing to respond to His appeal?

Nathan's Response

A young man in Allentown, Pennsylvania, had the courage to pray this radical prayer. Nathan worked in a foundry in Macungie, Pennsylvania. Just a few months before I met him, God had miraculously saved his life. He had accidentally put his hand on a live conduit at work, and 440 volts of electricity had surged through his body. He should have died that night. When the doctors examined him, they found the entry point of the electricity on his hand, but they couldn't find an exit point. Try to explain that. I can't. God miraculously spared Nathan's life that night for a reason. A few months later he knelt with me under the starry heavens and prayed a radical prayer. In his own words he cried out, "Lord of the harvest, I earnestly beg You to throw out laborers into Your harvest, and You have my permission to begin with *me.*" The young man prayed in simple faith, and God heard his prayer.

As a result, the Lord set into motion a sequence of events that would change his life forever. First God asked him to part with his most cherished possession: a BMW motorcycle. He loved that machine, even though Satan had tried to use it to end his life, urging him to take a suicidal ride on back roads at more than 100 miles per hour. When Nathan became convicted that God wanted him to part with his beloved BMW, he found the courage to let it go. His radical prayer was being answered.

Then God answered it further through the lives of other followers of Jesus. The Spirit of God moved two families in his home church to help sponsor Nathan to go to college. Those families made significant financial sacrifices to join the Lord of the harvest in throwing a laborer out into His harvest. One of those sponsors sleeps in Jesus today, but before he died he laid up some treasure in heaven.

Four years after Nathan, a former foundry employee, offered that radical prayer, he graduated from college with a degree in theology and as president of his senior class. Today Nathan is still a devoted follower of Jesus. He is serving as a local church pastor and is deeply committed to mission work. In fact, it was on one of those mission trips that he met his beautiful wife. God always gives us more than we deserve! Do you think Nathan regrets praying that radical prayer? No! Now, instead of just making a living, he is making a difference in the world.

Your Response

I'm not suggesting that everyone who prays this radical prayer will become a pastor. Rather, I'm simply encouraging you to see what it will allow the Lord of the harvest to do in your life. I challenge you to cry out to Him today and every day. Say to Him, "Whatever You want me to do, I'll do it. Wherever You want me to go, I'll go. If You want me to enter into a full-time ministry, I'm willing. Should You desire that I be a laborer for You at my work, at my business, in my home, I'm willing,

Lord. Or if You need me to give sacrificially to help send other laborers into Your harvest, I'm willing. Just show me what You want me to do, Lord. I give You full permission. I yield fully to You. Throw out laborers into Your harvest, and You have my permission to begin with *me.*"

Will you respond to Jesus' appeal? Will you offer this radical prayer? If you do pray it in faith, you will find your life transformed. However, I must warn you. You will also encounter radical challenges.

4

Encountering Radical Challenges

Whenever you pray the radical prayer, giving the Lord of the harvest permission to send you into His harvest, you will experience radical joy. However, you will also encounter powerful challenges. Jesus warned: "Behold, I send you out as lambs among wolves" (Luke 10:3). That sounds dangerous! But Jesus is painfully honest with you. When you cry out to the Lord of the harvest to become part of His harvest, you need to be prepared to face almost anything. Those radical challenges will be both internal and external.

Internal Challenges

An immediate one that many of us must confront is our lack of maturity and experience in God's work. We are just lambs. Sheep aren't known to be the most intelligent or the strongest members of the animal kingdom. But many of us aren't even fully grown sheep—just weak, immature lambs. We have heard the promise of Jesus when He said, "Greater works than these he will do, because I go to my Father" (John 14:12). Although we may believe the promise in theory, not many of us have ever tested it in real life. When you give the Lord of the harvest permission to throw you out into His harvest, you may come face to face with the painful realization that you are just a lamb. Joining the Lord of the harvest in His harvest is a radical challenge for lambs.

Wilbur was just a lamb when he gave the Lord of the harvest permission to use him. He had been a Christian all his life, but he was immature and inexperienced as a worker in the Lord's harvest. In March 2002 he received an invitation to preach a series of sermons in Kenya, Africa. His reply was terse and to the point: "You know I don't preach!" He could just as well have said, "I'm just a lamb! Choose a mature sheep like Billy Graham!" Surely God would select someone more experienced, more spiritually mature, than him. But Wilbur decided to ask God for a sign. After all, Gideon had asked for one to know whether it was indeed the Lord who was directing him to lead the army of Israel. So Wilbur knelt in prayer and said, "God, I have never asked for a sign before, but I need to know that this is what You want me to do." Immediately these words came to his mind: *Why are you requesting a sign? I have asked you to go into all the world, and I will be with you!* The answer was so clear. All this 70-plus-year-old "lamb" could say was "Thank You, Lord."

A few weeks later Wilbur e-mailed the local coordinator in Kenya and asked, "How many do you think will be attending the meetings?" The response shocked him. They expected approximately 5,000 people during the week and more than 10,000 on the weekends. When Wilbur read those numbers, he again confronted the painful realization that he was just a "lamb." He said to his wife, "There is no way that I could face that many people and preach those sermons." Wilbur wanted to serve God. He was willing to pray the radical prayer, giving the Lord of the harvest permission to throw him out into His harvest. But he was struggling with the radical internal challenge of being an immature and inexperienced lamb. Many of us can relate to his sense of inadequacy.

"Behold, I send you out as lambs among wolves."

External Challenges

Perhaps more frightening than the internal challenges are the external challenges: "Behold, I send you out as lambs *among wolves.*" Not only does God send you out as a lamb, but also you find yourself dispatched as a lamb among wolves. You will face adversaries when the Lord of the harvest throws you out into His harvest. Many of them will be predators. Such adversaries are not mild-mannered or timid. They are wolves that Jesus described as "ravenous" (Matt. 7:15). The apostle Paul called them "savage" (Acts 20:29). And notice that there is not just one wolf. Jesus said, "I send you out as lambs among wolves." Such predators hunt in packs. They look for vulnerable targets and seek to devour them.

The challenge is even more radical because of the fact that you go out *among* these ravenous, savage predators. It is not the nature of lambs to seek trouble. Lambs do not go wolf spotting or wolf hunting. Rather, *wolves* search for lambs. When you give the Lord of the harvest permission to use you in His harvest, there will be times that you will find yourself surrounded by these snarling, ravenous wolves.

Practical Wisdom

To meet such overpowering difficulties, both internal and external, you must heed the counsel of Jesus recorded in

Matthew 10:16. Speaking to the twelve, He says: "Behold, I send you out as sheep in the midst of wolves. Therefore, be wise as serpents and harmless as doves." The Greek word translated here as "wise" refers to practical wisdom, discernment, and prudence. It is the same wisdom that Jesus calls for at the end of His sermon on the mount (Matt. 7:24). The same Greek word frequently appears in the Greek translation of the book of Proverbs. Such practical wisdom helps us to know when to be silent (Prov. 11:12), when to withdraw (Prov. 14:16), and how to diffuse angry words (Prov. 15:1).

You need practical wisdom when God throws you out as a lamb among wolves. But what does Jesus mean when He says "Be wise as serpents"? The ancient Near East considered the serpent as a symbol of wisdom and cunning. Serpents are alert and cautious. They do not seek unnecessary contact or conflict with a predator, nor do they provoke attacks.

Purity and Faithfulness

When you find yourself out in the Lord's harvest as a lamb

among wolves, you also need to be as harmless as a dove. The Greek word translated "harmless" literally means "unmixed." The same word also describes pure gold. Laborers in the Lord's harvest are to demonstrate moral purity and integrity.

The ancient Near East regarded the dove as a symbol of purity and faithfulness. God summons you in your interaction with others, including the savage and ravenous wolves, to be above reproach in speech and conduct. The apostle Paul admonishes us: "Do not be overcome by evil, but overcome evil with good" (Rom. 12:21). Laborers in the Lord's harvest should never adopt the ethics or mimic the behaviors of their adversaries. Like the dove, you are a symbol of peace, hope, and the presence of God's Holy Spirit in a world filled with savage wolves.

The Example of Jesus

Jesus demonstrated wisdom in His interactions with His adversaries. Many of the religious leaders continually sought ways to trap Jesus and to destroy Him. Thus Jesus was a perfect example of a "lamb among wolves." He manifested a wisdom that comes from heaven by avoiding confrontation. On many occasions He realized that if He spoke the truth openly, His enemies would pounce on Him, accuse Him of blasphemy, and attempt to annihilate Him. Therefore, He taught in parables, so that His adversaries would see but not perceive, and hear but not understand (Matt. 13:10-13).

"Do not be overcome by evil, but overcome evil with good" (Rom. 12:21).

Immediately after Jesus cleansed the Temple, the religious leaders tried to trap Him by demanding, "By what authority are You doing these things?" (Matt. 21:23). If Jesus had answered them plainly, they would have surely stoned Him for blasphemy. It was true that Jesus had cleansed the Temple by His own authority as the Son of God, the Word made flesh. But He showed wisdom in His response to the religious leaders confronting Him when He said: "I also will ask you one thing, which if you tell Me, I likewise will tell you by what authority I do these things: 'The baptism of John—where was it from?

From heaven or from men?'" (verses 24, 25). In other words, "You answer My question, and I will answer yours." It threw the proverbial ball back into their court. Now the religious leaders faced a dilemma of their own. If they said John's baptism was from heaven, then they would be condemning themselves, because they had refused to listen to him. On the other hand, if they said the desert evangelist's baptism had a human origin, then the multitude would mob them, because people widely regarded John as a divinely inspired prophet. After conferring together, the religious leaders responded, "We do not know." Jesus then said to them, "Neither will I tell you by what authority I do these things" (verse 27).

You need similar practical wisdom when dealing with the

wolves that will inevitably surround you. But remember that such insight and understanding comes only from above. James reminds us that "if any of you lacks wisdom, let him ask of God, who gives to all *liberally* and without reproach, and it will be given to him" (James 1:5). The Lord of the harvest does not rebuke His lambs for their lack of maturity and experience. Rather, He encourages them to seek the practical wisdom that all of us will surely need to meet the radical challenges that we will encounter. He even offers to give us that practical wisdom liberally when we ask Him.

Useful Lambs

Perhaps you are wondering how a lamb such as Wilbur survived after he was thrown out into the faraway country of Kenya. In spite of internal and external challenges, he faithfully preached night after night, and when he gave his first invitation for people to accept

Jesus Christ as Savior and Lord, more than 400 people surged forward. He was totally amazed. The final weekend of the meetings had an estimated attendance of more than 25,000, and nearly 2,000 individuals made commitments to become fully devoted followers of Jesus.

But their hearts were willing, and God blessed their labors.

Wilbur learned by experience a lesson that we all need to acquire. When we give the Lord of the harvest permission to throw us out into His harvest, we may be as lambs among wolves, encountering seemingly insurmountable obstacles both inside and outside us, but we are not alone. Jesus is with us. He will never leave us or forsake us!

That's a lesson our son Christopher learned when he was a young teenager. One Sabbath afternoon he decided to go downtown with some friends to sing Christian songs and talk to people about Jesus. Without any experience with street witnessing, they were just lambs. But their hearts were willing, and God blessed their labors. Partway through the afternoon Christopher needed to use the men's room. While he was washing his hands, an older teenager came in and began to attack him verbally. "You're stupid! I think it's stupid to love Jesus!" Although Christopher felt intimidated, he replied, "I love Jesus!" Suddenly the door of one of the stalls opened, and a very large man emerged. More than six feet tall, he must have weighed at least 300 pounds. Walking up behind the older teenager, he said, "I love Jesus!" Startled, the aggressive teenager left—like a wolf with his tail between his legs! Our son Christopher had never met the stranger before, and he has never seen him since. But I have no doubt that God used that man to remind our son that even though you're just a lamb among wolves, you don't need to be afraid. Jesus will never leave you or forsake you!

"You're stupid!

I think it's stupid

to love Jesus!"

Can the Lord of the harvest use "lambs" to do His work, even in the midst of hostile wolves? Absolutely! But we must learn to labor in radical dependence on the Lord of the harvest.

5

Laboring in Radical Dependence

When you give the Lord of the harvest permission to involve you in His harvest, as a lamb among wolves, He asks you to demonstrate an attitude of radical dependence. "Carry neither money bag, knapsack, nor sandals" (Luke 10:4).

Radical Instructions

His instructions don't make much sense from a human perspective. When you go on a journey, it is customary to take provisions with you. Experienced travelers advise you to take more money than you think you'll need! But Jesus gives the exact opposite advice: "Carry no money bag." In His directions to the twelve, Jesus is even more specific: "Provide neither gold nor silver nor copper" (Matt. 10:9).

Why does Jesus tell His followers to carry no money bag? Surely when you participate in the Lord's harvest you will need resources in order to accomplish your mission. Doesn't such an approach seem a little careless or irresponsible? Apparently, the Lord of the harvest doesn't want you to depend on your own ability. Rather, He seeks for you to labor in total dependence on Him.

Crisis in Sweden

During the summer between my junior and senior years of college I learned a vital lesson about radical dependence on the Lord of the harvest. I had traveled to Sweden to plant trees, having carefully designed my summer work plans to accomplish my personal goals for the coming year. But the Lord of the harvest invaded my private world and challenged me to allow Him to throw me out into His harvest.

Through a remarkable sequence of events I found myself in the north of Sweden, selling Christian books. That was the last possible kind of thing I would have ever considered doing for the summer. But the Lord of the harvest had other plans. I memorized a brief sales presentation in Swedish and started knocking on doors. To my surprise, the first few days went well. The families that I visited took pity on me. By the end of my first week of sales I began to feel rather self-confident—even haughty. That's when my troubles began.

The following Monday I worked for 10 hours and sold nothing—not one single book. "These people have problems," I said to myself, blaming the local residents when I should have been looking in a mirror. I worked all day Tuesday without any success. By Wednesday morning I had lost all my self-confidence. I was so discouraged that when I knocked on the doors I secretly hoped that no one was home. It was pitiful!

Thoroughly dejected, I finally sat down on the side of the road in a very exclusive housing development in the north of Sweden and began complaining to the Lord of the harvest: "Lord, I can't do this! I can't even give these books away!" By now I felt a complete failure. What I didn't realize was that in reality I was on the verge of making a major breakthrough in my relationship with God.

"But if You want to work through me, Lord, I'm willing!"

"Lord," I continued, "I know You brought me here for a reason. I have sensed Your leading. But I can't do this work." Then I hesitantly added, "But if You want to work through me, Lord, I'm willing!" It was a simple prayer—a confession of radical dependence on the Lord of the harvest.

Radical Dependence

The Lord of the harvest invites you to depend totally and unreservedly upon Him. If you are trusting your own resources, you might not even give the Lord of the harvest permission to involve you at all. You might say to yourself, "As soon as I have what I need for such an enormous task, then I'll give You permission to use me." Or you might allow the Lord of the harvest to include you, but then look for a small task to do that seems manageable with your meager ability. In order to emphasize the need for radical dependence on the Lord of the harvest, Jesus instructs you to leave your money bag behind.

In addition to abandoning your money bag, Jesus also directs you not to carry a "knapsack" (Luke 10:4). What is this knapsack that we should leave behind? The Greek word translated "knapsack" (NKJV), "scrip" (KJV), or "bag" (NIV) occurs only six times in the New Testament. Each reference, including the passage in Luke 10:4, deals with going out as laborers into the Lord's harvest. Is this knapsack the equivalent of a twenty-first-century rolling suitcase? Is Jesus simply saying, "Don't take any money and don't bring along any luggage"? I don't think so. This Greek noun has a more specialized meaning—a beggar's bag. According to the writings of the Hellenistic philosopher Crates of Thebes, itinerant teachers carried such beggar's bags with them. Jesus, however, asks His followers to leave the beggar's bag behind. We are not to beg from others. Radical dependence on the Lord of the harvest means first that we don't trust in our own resources and second that we don't impose on those around us to supply what we need.

Even at the time of the sending out of the 70, the Lord of the harvest had already demonstrated His ability to provide. "When I sent you without money bag, knapsack, and sandals, did you lack anything?" He asked them (Luke 22:35). "Nothing," they replied. The disciples did not rely on their own resources or impose on those around them. Rather, they demonstrated radical dependence on the Lord of the harvest, and as a result they lacked nothing. God will also supply the resources you need in His harvest as you labor in radical dependence on Him.

The Lord of the Harvest Will Provide

How then will the Lord of the harvest meet your needs? He has a thousand ways to care for you as you labor in total dependence on Him! One way the Lord of the harvest will provide for you is through the generosity of those whose hearts are willing. If a family offers hospitality to you, not because you begged, but because the Lord of the harvest touched their hearts, Jesus says, "Remain in the same house, eating and drinking such things as they give, for the laborer is worthy of his wages. Do not go from house to house" (Luke 10:7). Accept what the Lord of the harvest supplies you. Don't go from house to house looking for a better offer. Be content with the resources provided.

The patriarch Abraham gave the Lord permission to throw him out of his hometown of Ur. The author of the book of Hebrews tells us that Abraham "went out, not knowing where he was going" (Heb. 11:8). The patriarch realized that this world was not his final resting place. He was waiting "for the city which has foundations, whose builder and maker is God" (verse 10). On his life journey Abraham came to know the Lord God as YHWH-yireh, "The-Lord-Will-Provide" (Gen. 22:14). That can also be your experience as you labor in radical dependence on the Lord of the harvest.

He provides salvation through Jesus Christ our Lord (Rom. 10:9, 13) and power and guidance through the presence and ministry of the Holy Spirit (Acts 1:8; John 16:13). And the Lord of the harvest will supply all of your other needs "according to His riches in glory by Christ Jesus" (Phil. 4:19). As you labor in radical dependence on Him, you will discover personally that He will sustain you in every possible way!

Travel Light and Stay Focused

Jesus also reminds laborers in the harvest not to get bogged down with excess baggage. The instruction to carry no sandals (Luke 10:4) doesn't mean that laborers should be barefoot. Jesus doesn't say, "Don't wear sandals," but "Carry no sandals." In other words: "Don't be burdened down with excess baggage." The verb translated "carry" literally means to "bear a burden." It's the same verb that Scripture uses for bearing a cross. Carrying an extra pair of sandals may not seem like much of a burden, much of a hindrance. However, in addition to an extra pair of sandals, you might decide to take more clothes and another walking stick. Carry no (extra) sandals. Travel light. Don't be bogged down with excess baggage.

As you travel on your journey, Jesus also directs you to "greet no one along the road" (verse 4). Does He want his followers to be antisocial? No! It is a hyperbole—an exaggeration for effect. Jesus is saying, "Don't get distracted. Stay focused on your mission." Similarly, He told those who would be His disciples, "Don't even go back and say goodbye to your family. Don't look back once you have put your hands to the plow" (Luke 9:62, paraphrase). Let nothing come between you and your mission.

Don't look back once you have put your hands to the plow" (Luke 9:62

The Mission

What, then, is your mission as a laborer in the Lord's harvest? "Heal the sick there, and say to them, 'The kingdom of God has come near to you'" (Luke 10:9). Previously Jesus had given these instructions to the twelve: "As you go, preach, saying, 'The kingdom of heaven is at hand.' Heal the sick, cleanse the lepers, raise the dead, cast out demons. Freely you have received, freely give" (Matt. 10:7, 8).

Did you notice that the mission assignment given to those who are involved in the Lord's harvest is also a description of Christ's own ministry while He was here on earth? In the report sent to John the Baptist, Jesus said, "Go and tell John the things which you hear and see: The blind see and the lame walk; the lepers are cleansed and the deaf hear; the dead are raised up and the poor have the gospel preached to them" (Matt. 11:4, 5). Such ministry was possible only because, as Jesus testified: "The Spirit of the Lord is upon Me, because He has anointed Me to preach the gospel to the poor; He has sent Me to heal the brokenhearted, to proclaim liberty to the captives and recovery of sight to the blind, to set at liberty those who are oppressed; to proclaim the acceptable year of the Lord" (Luke 4:18, 19).

He calls us, as laborers in the Lord's harvest, to demonstrate radical dependence as we reproduce the ministry of Jesus, walk in His footsteps, and serve in His name. It is not by might or by power but by God's Spirit that the harvest will be gathered in. Jesus testified: "But you shall receive power when the Holy Spirit has come upon you; and you shall be witnesses to Me in Jerusalem, and in all Judea and Samaria, and to the end of the earth" (Acts 1:8). Only as we have freely received can we freely give. We give to others in constant awareness of our radical dependence on the Lord of the harvest.

Miraculous Provision

As I sat on the side of the road in that exclusive housing development in the north of Sweden, I was painfully aware of my own inadequacies. I had tried to rely on my own wisdom and strength, and I had failed miserably. But after I prayed a simple prayer of surrender—a radical prayer giving God permission to assign me to His harvest—He began to work in a miraculous manner. I got up from the side of the road and made my way to the next house. When the woman opened the front door, I sensed in my heart that the Holy Spirit had been there ahead of me. She bought a set of books. And that story repeated itself again and again during the next five weeks.

Several days after I prayed the radical prayer and made the commitment to labor in radical dependence on the Lord of the harvest, I experienced another miracle. At one home I felt impressed to give my testimony. That may not sound unusual to you, but may I remind you that I didn't speak Swedish. However, as I responded to the conviction of God's Spirit, something remarkable happened to me. I felt a freedom to begin communi-

cating in a language I had not studied and did not speak. I gave my testimony—in Swedish! Perhaps you're thinking, *How do you know you were speaking Swedish?* Because she obviously understood what I was saying. God supplied me the gift of tongues, and He endowed her with the gift of understanding.

Only as we have freely received can we freely give.

He is YHWH-yireh, Jehovah-jireh! When I left that house, I was convinced beyond any shadow of a doubt that the Lord of the harvest was able to do more than I could even ask or think of, if I was only willing to labor in radical dependence on Him.

God will not supply everyone in the same way. But when you make a commitment to allow the Lord of the harvest to put you in the service of His harvest, and labor in radical dependence on Him, you too will witness His remarkable provisions as He works in you and through you. And believe me, when that happens, you will experience radical joy!

6

Experiencing Radical Joy

Can you imagine how the disciples felt when they returned from their first missionary tour? They had given the Lord of the harvest permission to enroll them in His harvest labors. Even though they felt like lambs among wolves, they had learned to depend in a radical way upon Him. Each had experienced that He is Jehovah-jireh, "The-Lord-Will-Provide." They healed the sick in Jesus' name and set those in bondage free as they boldly proclaimed the good news about Jesus. Luke records that "the seventy returned with joy" (Luke 10:17).

Whenever you labor in the Lord's harvest, you can be certain that you too will return with a joyful testimony. Your own life will also be transformed as you allow God to work in you and through you. The following testimonies come from individuals who have given the Lord of the harvest permission to assign them in His harvest. Yes, they encountered radical challenges, but as they labored in radical dependence on the Lord of that harvest, they also experienced radical joy. Perhaps you will see yourself in one of these stories.

Mary Ann's Story

Mary Ann Roberts grew up in a Christian home, but as a young person she never made a personal commitment to Jesus as her Savior and Lord. After college she married, her husband joined the military, and they moved to Europe. It was there that Mary Ann abandoned all connections with church and became a self-described party animal.

During 1983 she hit rock bottom. In the midst of a weekend-long drinking binge she became so drunk and sick that she was unable to attend a family reunion. That's when Mary Ann decided to ask God back into her life. The vivid picture that came to her mind at that low point in her life was of a loving Father running down the road to meet His prodigal child. Mary Ann knew she was that child.

Realizing that she needed to make some radical changes in her lifestyle, she wrote to a Christian pastor and told him of her commitment to become a follower of Jesus. That pastor's wife understood how difficult the transition would be and supported Mary Ann by calling her on the telephone every single morning for an entire year to pray with her.

Even though Mary Ann started attending a Christian church and God became a vital part of her life, she sensed that something was still missing—that God had something special in store for her that she had not yet found. Since she had always wished that she had continued her education, she decided to go back to school. Perhaps it would fill the void in her heart. She applied to and was accepted into a graduate program in science and eventually completed a Ph.D. in neuroscience. But somehow life still seemed incomplete.

In the summer of 2001 Mary Ann attended a camp meeting in North Carolina. She was interested mainly in socializing with friends, so she sat near the back of the auditorium.

"Lord, I give You permission to throw me out into Your harvest."

During one of the meetings, though, she overheard a Christian evangelist invite those who were interested in a ministry project in Kenya to meet with him after the service.

"Usually I like to mull things over before I act," Mary Ann recalls, "but it was as if someone were standing in front of me and pointing directly at me." At the close of the meeting she walked up to the front of the auditorium under deep conviction that God was calling her to participate in the ministry project in Kenya. After talking with her, the evangelist invited her to conduct a series of meetings in the primitive community of Rongo, Kenya. Mary Ann was not a public speaker. She had no homiletical training and absolutely no experience in frontline mission work. It had never even crossed her mind that God would ask her to become a preacher. But she was open to the working of the Holy Spirit that day, and, in her own words, she began to pray the radical prayer: "Lord, I give You permission to throw me out into Your harvest."

The Lord of the harvest loves to hear that prayer. And more than that, He loves to answer it. God took Mary Ann and threw her out into His great harvest in Kenya. But just as soon as she arrived in Rongo, she began encountering radical challenges, both internal and external. First she discovered that the roads in the area were bad—almost impassable. That would make it difficult for people to attend the meetings. Then she learned that the two other volunteers who were supposed to serve as part of her team weren't going to show up. How would you have felt?

Mary Ann found herself completely alone in her hotel room, thousands of miles away from home, preparing to do something she had never done before—preach. She was terrified! The multitude of internal and external challenges seemed overwhelming. So what did she do? Give up? No! She knew about YHWH-yireh, Jehovah-jireh, and cried out to the Lord of the harvest. "I told the Lord how scared I was," she recounts, "and then I read Isaiah 41:10. As I read those words of the Lord, I held up my right hand, and I felt His presence. It was incredible! I felt no fear."

Every day Mary Ann prepared a new message, and every night she shared it in radical dependence on the Lord of the harvest. Whenever she stood up and began her talk, she sensed God speaking through her to the crowd assembled in the town square. At the end of those meetings in Rongo, Kenya, more than 500 people confessed their love for Jesus in baptism. As you can imagine, Mary Ann was filled with joy— radical joy!

That radical joy has not dissipated. As a result of allowing the Lord of the harvest to involve her in His great labor, the focus of her life is completely different now. And if you meet her, you'll realize that she wants every person she connects with to have a personal relationship with Jesus.

Mary Ann made a subsequent trip to Africa, this time to Rwanda, and was able to share the good news about Jesus with an audience of nearly 5,000 people every night. Those meetings were unique because nearly all of those present had lost family members in the genocide of the 1990s. She recounts that at the conclusion of one of her messages, the entire audience surged to the front in response to her appeal. It seemed as if everyone present wanted to know Jesus. The whole group began singing, "We're going to the New Jerusalem." As Mary Ann witnessed that scene, she felt filled with what the apostle Peter calls a "joy inexpressible and full of glory" (1 Peter 1:8). Real joy! Radical joy!

Today she continues to give God permission to use her in His harvest, and in spite of facing great challenges, she has a joyful testimony!

Wintley's Story

Wintley Phipps is another incredible example of someone who has given God permission to use him as a laborer in His great harvest.

As a 5-year-old growing up in Trinidad, Wintley imagined himself traveling to faraway places. He had a little red tricycle that he would turn on its side and, using one of the back wheels as a steering wheel, sit and dream for hours that he was flying and driving to places where he would meet important people.

When Wintley was a teenager, his dreams turned to music. That was during the Woodstock and pop rock era. He thought that if he could just be part of Sly and the Family Stone he would see his dreams fulfilled. When he was about 15 years old, Wintley actually got to meet Sly Stone and Tom Jones. It was a profound experience for him, but also a terrible disappointment as he realized that such musical performers weren't happy. The men had everything materially, but they had no peace or contentment.

A turning point in Wintley's life came when he was a 16-year-old boarding student at a Christian school in Ontario, Canada. One day he went to the dean and said, "I'm sorry. I can't take all of these rules and regulations. I'm leaving this school."

"Is that what you really want to do?" the dean asked.

"That's right," Wintley replied.

"God, whatever You want me to do, I'll do it."

Then the dean looked at him and said, "Why don't you do for once not what you want to do but what *God* wants you to do?"

Those words hit the young man like a freight train. He thought about them all the way back to his dorm room. There he got down on his knees and prayed, "God, whatever You want me to do, I'll do it. If You want me to be a garbage man, and the only music I'll ever know is whistling hymns on the back of a garbage truck, that's fine with me." Then he added, "God, You know I'd like to travel—to use my talents for You.

If that's Your will for me, open up the doors and let me see Your leading." Wintley didn't realize it, but in his own words he was praying the radical prayer.

The following day two men walked up to him and said, "Are you Wintley Phipps? We are from a singing group called the Heritage Family, and we would like you to travel and do singing evangelism with us."

Never having seen a prayer answered like that before, Wintley was speechless. He came under conviction that God had a special plan and that He was going to answer his prayer. A few days later a deep spiritual impression came to him as he walked across campus. God impressed Wintley with the thought *If you can just be faithful, I'm going to allow your life to go down an unusual path. It will allow you the opportunity to speak truth to those in power, and I want you to prepare to articulate the issues of religious freedom.* With that personal spiritual mandate, Wintley entered into what would be his life's ministry.

The Lord of the harvest has given him the opportunity to be a witness for Jesus around the world. Wintley remembers a phone call that he received from the father of Stephen Oake. Stephen had been a British police officer that a terrorist had stabbed to death in Manchester, England. His death rocked the whole nation. Oake's father called Wintley and asked him if he would sing at his son's funeral. Representatives from the royal family were there. Prime minister Tony Blair sat on the front row. Wintley had the privilege of ministering to all present.

During a visit to Viti Levu, the main island of the Fiji islands, Wintley was standing in a hotel lobby in Suva when two men walked up to him. "Are you Wintley Phipps?" they inquired. "You sang at the National Prayer Breakfast last year. We were there as representatives of our country." Later they phoned Wintley at the hotel and said, "The prime minister would like you to come over to his home." It was his father's birthday, and they asked Wintley to sing for the occasion.

Then, after Wintley did, the prime minister announced, "We want to sing for *you!*" The prime minister handed out songbooks to all of his cabinet, and then they began to sing for Wintley! It was a glorious moment, filling Wintley's heart with joy. Radical joy.

On another occasion he was singing in Baltimore, Maryland. When he came down off the platform, a young woman stood waiting for him. "Sir, I just heard you sing, and I'm really discouraged," she told him. She was about to be fired from her job. "I feel as if I can talk to you," she continued. "Do you have time?" Wintley said, "Sure."

That young woman started visiting Phipps' home, and they would pray together. After praying with her one day, he said to her, "Before you go today, God has impressed me to tell you that He's going to bless you. He is going to give you the opportunity to speak to millions of people."

"Do you think that God would do that for me?" she asked.

The history of her life demonstrates that the answer to her question was yes! She went on to become an internationally known communicator and philanthropist, impacting millions of lives around the globe. Through the years God has given Wintley the opportunity to have a friendship with one of the most influential individuals of our generation.

The Lord has arranged many opportunities for Wintley to provide counsel. One such instance presented itself during the Monica Lewinsky scandal. The Lord impressed Phipps to send President Clinton a message. "Mr. President, read Psalm 69." Some time later Wintley attended another function at the White House, and one of President Clinton's cabinet members called him aside and said, "You don't know what happened, do you? The president read that psalm. He called a few of his closest cabinet members together and shared with us from Psalm 69. Then President Clinton went to his room and wrote out the first speech that he would give to the American people admitting he had

"I want you to prepare to articulate the issues of religious freedom."

sinned." Wintley was asked to be in the audience at the White House when President Clinton presented that speech. That day Phipps remembered the Lord's promise to him many years before that He would take his life down an unusual path and that he would speak truth to powerful people.

Several years ago as he rode an elevator at Capitol Hill a man from the back of the elevator said, "Wintley Phipps, I want you to know that your music has been a blessing to my life." It was Senator Sam Brownback of Kansas. "Tomorrow in the Rotunda," he continued, "we are giving Mother Teresa the Congressional Gold Medal. Would you come and close the program tomorrow with 'Amazing Grace'?" It was probably the last time Mother Teresa heard the hymn. She died not long afterward. Wintley will never forget seeing Mother Teresa beckon her aide and come over to hug him and thank him for singing that song. It filled his heart with joy. Radical joy.

God continues to bless abundantly his life and work. Radical joy has overwhelmed his life as he continues to allow God to throw him into the labor of His harvest.

Rachel's Story

Unlike Mary Ann, Rachel didn't wait until she was older to give the Lord of the harvest permission to use her as His harvest laborer. From her very first year at a Christian university, Rachel made a commitment to serve as a student missionary. Four years later she realized her dream. Directly after graduation Rachel traveled to Monteverde, Costa Rica, as a volunteer teacher in a small Christian school.

But before she even left for Costa Rica, she began to encounter great challenges. The friend who was supposed to serve with her in Monteverde had a family crisis and couldn't go. Rachel wondered whether she should just stay home too, but she sensed the Lord of the harvest speaking to her heart: *Go. Trust Me, and go.* She obeyed, allowing Him to throw her out into His harvest.

When she arrived in Costa Rica, she faced more difficulties. First, she waited more than an hour and a half at the airport, and no one arrived to meet her. Then she realized that she didn't even know the address of her final destination, and she had no contact phone numbers at the school. It was a time either to become hysterical or to demonstrate radical dependence on the Lord of the harvest.

Finally, Rachel connected with a young man who transported her to the mission school. But when she got to the school, she encountered more challenges. It had no director to talk to and no real program in place for volunteers. Someone sat her down and, with the help of a translator, said, "We don't have an English program at all! So we want you to develop one, right now!"

Rachel felt completely overwhelmed! Because she had been told that a complete English program was already in place, she had not brought any resources with her. She had one week to plan an entire English language program and didn't even know where to begin.

"It was all too big for me to handle," Rachel admits, "but God reminded me that He had brought me here and that no matter what happened, I was here for His purposes." Then she remembered a statement from a Life and Teachings of Jesus class: "If the plan isn't big enough to scare you, it's not big enough for God."

In spite of many radical challenges, the Lord of the harvest provided for her. After several months of struggling, Rachel connected with a wonderful Christian teacher named Lindy, who lived in a nearby town. Lindy was an amazing woman of God who had taught since she was 14 years old. She stepped in and helped Rachel design a very creative curriculum. Soon it was obvious to Rachel that her students were actually beginning to enjoy their lessons.

When she came home for a break halfway through her mission assignment, she diligently gathered extra teaching supplies to take back with her. The English program at the mission school was flourishing, but she determined to make it even better. However, when she returned to Monteverde after her break, she discovered that other staff members at the school had burned many of the books she had been using. They weren't trying to be malicious—they had just assumed that she would no longer need them. That's when Rachel concluded that the school needed a designated space especially for the English language program.

The campus had an unfinished building that a high school-age mission team had started. Rachel decided that in addition to her teaching responsibilities, she was going to supervise the completion of that building so that the English language program could have a home of its own. She wrote to her family, and they, along with members from her local church, assured her they would raise the $2,000 needed to complete that classroom as an English language lab.

"If the plan isn't big enough to scare you, it's not big enough for God."

But before any funds arrived from back home, Rachel had to move forward in complete dependence on the Lord. She found an honest local builder who put his other projects on hold and began to finish the building. But she had to pay the contractor from her own bank account—funds that she had saved from the past summer and that were supposed to last for the whole year. Rachel remembers the day she completely emptied her bank account. The promised money still hadn't arrived from back home. Even today she can still feel the tightness in her chest as she realized that she no longer had any money. No resources. All she could do was completely depend on the Lord of the harvest.

Before Rachel left Costa Rica, though, she was able to see that classroom completed. It was not only well built but beautiful. Shelving to store the new English language curriculum, along with all the books and supplies, covered one entire wall. The building even had a lock on the door so that no one could come in and burn the books!

Since returning home, Rachel has heard that the building still remains in use and that the English language program is continuing. As she reflects back on the experience, she says,

"There is no way that I did that! I couldn't have. I saw God make me an instrument in His hands. I had nothing to offer except my willingness. He took situations that were just too big for me and reminded me that I must look outward, away from myself and to Him, for answers and for strength." Rachel rejoices that the Lord of the harvest provided in miraculous ways during her time in Costa Rica, and she is filled with joy. Radical joy.

Rachel still allows God to use her at any time, in any place. She expressed her commitment this way: "Some people say that you should just make your plans and ask God to bless you. I don't want to live like that! I want God to make the plans." Recently Rachel has become involved in the leadership of a vibrant young adult Bible study group. "It wasn't my idea," she explains. "Someone just asked me to help lead the group, and I said yes." God has been blessing the young adult ministry in supernatural ways. Constantly Rachel notices that God is leading to the group young adults who are broken and hurting. At the same time He is also drawing other young adults who can offer love and support. The group is growing as people invite their friends.

Obviously Rachel is excited about what God is doing in the Bible study group. "We take time to study the Word of God, we take time for prayer, and we take time for connecting together. We truly care about one another. God is blessing, and I'm so glad to be part of it!" That's joy—radical joy!

When I met with Rachel to listen to her story, I heard her pray a beautiful prayer. She gave the Lord of the harvest permission, once again, to involve her in His harvest. I was reminded that praying the radical prayer is not just a once-in-a-lifetime event—it is a daily commitment. Rachel continues to experience radical joy as she labors in His harvest.

Githaka's Story

I first met Githaka Ngotho in the spring of 2002. The Lord had thrown both of us out into His harvest, and we ended up in the same little town of Kerugoya, Kenya. It was immediately apparent to me that Githaka was a devoted follower of Jesus, but I have recently learned more about the wonderful ways that God has been working in his life.

Githaka's father suffered greatly as a freedom fighter during the colonial era in Kenya, and his negative attitude toward Christianity greatly influenced the son. While still in high school, Githaka attended a revival week with some of his classmates. At the end of one of the services the preacher invited people to come to the front of the hall. As people fell down on the floor, uttering strange sounds, Githaka just stood there. Then the preacher came over to him, shook his head in an uncomfortable way, and said, "Just imitate the others!" At that point Githaka walked out of the meeting and never went back.

After completing high school, he returned home and discovered that a Christian evangelist was holding some meetings in his hometown. In spite of the lack of support from his parents, Githaka decided to attend. At the end of that series he confessed his love for Jesus in baptism. Following his baptism, Githaka became actively involved in a local church. He visited people who were interested in studying the Bible, and served as a youth leader. Occasionally he even received an opportunity to preach a sermon. Githaka experienced joy as he helped people to know Jesus.

A turning point in his life came in the spring of 2002. That was when I first met him. I was scheduled to conduct meetings in a town not far from his home. When the assigned translator failed to show up, Githaka offered to help. He gave the Lord of the harvest permission to make him a laborer in His harvest.

We worked together like an experienced team. Sometimes I felt that Githaka was preaching a more powerful sermon than I was! However, I was totally unaware of some of the radical challenges he was struggling with during those meetings. He had no accommodations and, for several days, little to eat. And yet Githaka labored with a joyful spirit, never complaining. I'm not sure that he ever prayed the radical prayer with words. But he clearly prayed it with his life during those three weeks. "Lord of the harvest, I earnestly beg You to throw out laborers into Your harvest, and You have my permission to begin with me."

He gave the Lord of the harvest permission to make him a laborer in His harvest.

During those meetings, as we were preaching together from night to night, he came under the deep conviction of the Holy Spirit: *This is the work for you!* Githaka was interested in the possibility of going to college to prepare for full-time ministry, but that brought up another enormous challenge that he faced. In his own words, he was "financially crippled." Yet having given permission for God to employ him in the divine harvest, Githaka was about to discover that its Lord is YHWH-yireh,

Jehovah-jireh. At the conclusion of those meetings a Christian family offered to sponsor him to prepare for the gospel ministry.

Today Githaka is a full-time pastor. He has a joyful testimony, in spite of the fact that he still faces great challenges. Because the church has very limited resources in the part of Kenya in which he serves as a pastor, Githaka receives no formal compensation. He labors in radical dependence on the Lord of the harvest.

Recently Githaka recounted another experience in which he had to depend fully on God. He once visited a home and was welcomed in by the wife and children. However, as soon as he sat down, a man appeared with a machete in his hand. Githaka assumed that he was the woman's husband. Three times the man pointed at him with the machete and then motioned toward the door, but Githaka remained motionless. "I am not a naturally brave person," Githaka confessed, "but Jesus gave me courage!" Finally the husband pointed to a chair and told him that he had 15 minutes to share with the family. Those 15 minutes turned into an hour Bible study, followed by a one-hour study three times a week. One month later, just before leaving the area, the entire family accepted Jesus as their personal Savior and Lord.

Githaka continues to give the Lord of the harvest permission to use him. As he does so, he experiences radical joy. Recently Githaka married a wonderful Christian woman named Happiness. What an appropriate companion for a courageous laborer who has prayed the radical prayer!

Bodil's Story

Radical joy is apparent on the face of Bodil Morris when she talks about what God has done in her life and ministry. She has prayed the radical prayer, giving the Lord of the harvest permission to involve her in His work. As a young mother of two small boys, she noticed the way that young minds soak up and retain words and tunes. She observed that she still remembered nursery rhymes from her own childhood even though she didn't consider herself to have a particularly good memory. That's when she made the commitment to begin composing Scripture songs so that she could "hide God's Word" in her own heart and in that of her two young sons, Christopher and Jonathan.

In order to be obedient to that conviction, Bodil had to overcome some radical challenges. She felt poorly prepared and inadequate for the task. Although she had taken music lessons as a child, she felt frustrated by her inability to sight-read notes quickly. "God has used my weaknesses," she testifies. He did not leave her to face those challenges alone. Shortly after she began composing Scripture songs, Bodil met a gifted young Christian vocalist named Ashley Hold. They began to sing God's Word together, and the ministry of Trilogy Scripture Songs came into being. In the past 20 years Bodil has composed more than 100 Scripture songs, and Trilogy Scripture Songs has produced six CDs of them. More than 200 Christian radio stations across North America now broadcast her songs. Her Web site, www.trilogyscripturesongs.com, has also enabled her to provide Scripture songs to countless families around the world.

Whenever Bodil hears testimonies from those whose lives the Word of God has transformed, it fills her heart with joy. Radical joy! An elementary school teacher at a Christian school in California shared the experience of one of her second graders. She had asked all of her students to memorize a passage of Scripture. One little boy was very unhappy about the assignment, though. He didn't like to memorize anything. But this assignment would be different. The teacher gave each of the students one of Bodil's Scripture songs CDs. It contained 18 Scripture songs from the sayings of Jesus. The teacher encouraged her students to listen to them and to fill their hearts with the Word of God. Not long afterward, the second grader returned and joyfully recited all 13 verses of Matthew 25:1-13. It was the longest passage of Scripture on the whole CD. What would have seemed like an impossible memorization assignment became a possibility when this second grader learned the Scripture song of the parable of the ten virgins. The Christian school teacher sent an e-mail testimony to the Trilogy Web site, reporting that the little boy had not only completed his memorization assignment but was doing better in all his other studies and had experienced personal transformation. Such testimonies can fill anyone's heart with joy. Radical joy!

The Scripture songs are also impacting whole Christian communities. A music ministry leader from a Christian church in Georgia reported: "We have given copies of your Scripture CDs to each family in our church and have been using the songs each week in our worship service. The melodies appeal to all age groups, and we love the fact that the lyrics are taken directly from Scripture. They have been a great blessing as we seek to hide God's Word in our hearts."

Bodil recognizes that she could not have accomplished such a powerful ministry by herself. She refers to Trilogy Scripture Songs as a "living example of the body of Christ working together for His glory." And she continues to experience radical joy as she allows the Lord of the harvest to make her His laborer.

The Rest of the Story

The testimonies of these five individuals confirm that whenever you accept the Lord of the harvest's call, you will have a joyful testimony when you return from serving Him. Just as with the first disciples of Jesus, you will experience joy—radical joy!

You bring radical joy to the heart of Jesus Himself.

Jesus concludes His teaching about the radical prayer by reminding us that we will find our greatest joy in a personal relationship with Him as our Savior and Lord. "Nevertheless do not rejoice in this, that the spirits are subject to you, but rather rejoice because your names are written in heaven" (Luke 10:20). Is it wrong to rejoice when we see the Lord of the harvest working through us in wonderful ways? Of course not! Here again Jesus is using hyperbole—an exaggeration to make a point. We can experience radical joy when we see the Lord of the harvest accomplishing wonderful things through us, but our greatest joy comes from knowing Jesus, whom to know is life eternal!

When you serve the Lord of the harvest, you also bring radical joy to the heart of Jesus Himself. Immediately after the teaching of Jesus about the radical prayer, Luke records: "In that hour Jesus rejoiced" (verse 21). That word translated "rejoiced" in the New King James Version is a strong verb in Greek. It literally means "much jumping." Jesus was jumping for joy! When you respond to the appeal of Jesus, giving God permission to harvest through you, He experiences radical joy

too. What a beautiful thought! I want to bring great joy to the heart of Jesus, don't you?

Your Story

Why not respond to Jesus' invitation right now? Pray the radical prayer, today and every day, until our Lord returns in glory:

"Lord of the harvest, I earnestly beg You to throw out laborers into Your harvest, and You have my permission to begin with *me.*"

Then share *your* testimony of radical joy!*

---

* You can share your testimony with others at *www.radicaljoy.com.* At that same Web site you can read the joyful testimonies of those who have already courageously responded to Jesus.